My First
CLASSICAL RECORDER BOOK

D1482146

Selected & Edited by
L. C. Harnsberger

Dedication
May this book inspire a love for classical music to musicians of all ages. The recorder is a perfect instrument to start a musical life. I was fortunate to have a mother who loved classical music and shared her love with me. This book is dedicated to her. In loving memory of Therese Coscarelli Harnsberger 1930–2001.

Contents

Copyright © MMII by Alfred Music
All rights reserved.   Produced in USA.
ISBN 0-7390-2457-4 (Book)
ISBN 0-7390-2458-2 (Book & Recorder)

Cover photos: Karen Miller
Interior illustrations: Christine Finn
Composer illustrations on cover, from left to right:
Ludwig van Beethoven, Johannes Brahms and
Johann Sebastian Bach

About the Recorder

The recorder was probably invented in Italy during the 14th century. It was most popular during the Renaissance period of music that lasted from 1450 to 1600. Recorders are often played alone as solo instruments, in groups with other instruments, or in groups of four to nine recorders called *consorts*.

Types of Recorders

There are four sizes of recorders commonly used today. From the highest-sounding to the lowest, they are the *soprano* (or descant), *alto*, *tenor* (or treble) and *bass*.

There are two others that are very rarely used: the *sopranino*, which is smaller and higher-sounding than the soprano; and the *big bass*, which is larger and sounds lower than the bass.

The soprano is the most common recorder used today. It is best to start learning with this recorder before playing any of the others.

big bass

bass

tenor

alto

soprano

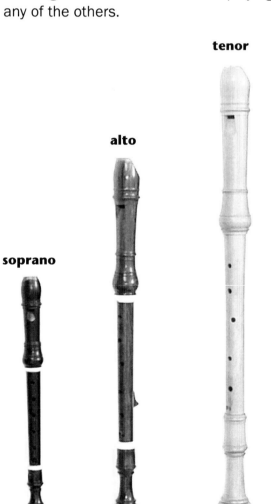

sopranino

Parts of the Recorder

Although some recorders are made of one single piece, many are made up of three pieces that fit snugly together. The top is called the *head*; the middle is called the *barrel*, and the bottom is called the *bell*.

The very top of the head is called the mouthpiece which is the part of the recorder into which you blow.

Care of the Recorder

Each time you finish playing, it is important to run a swab through the recorder to dry all the moisture. A small piece of towel attached to a stick will work well. If you have a three-piece recorder, you may need to occasionally apply a small amount of cork grease to keep the sections from sticking together.

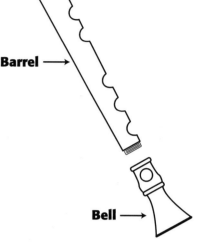

Mouthpiece →

Head →

Barrel →

Bell →

Holding the Recorder

When holding the recorder, it is important to use the center of your fingers to cover each hole, keeping the fingers as flat as possible (see photo). It is not correct to cover the holes with just the tips of the fingers.

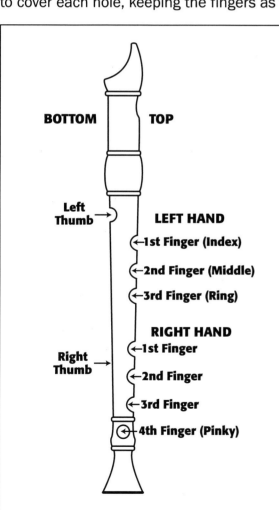

BOTTOM   TOP

Left Thumb →

LEFT HAND
←1st Finger (Index)
←2nd Finger (Middle)
←3rd Finger (Ring)

RIGHT HAND
←1st Finger
Right Thumb →
←2nd Finger
←3rd Finger
←4th Finger (Pinky)

Playing the Recorder

Be sure not to put any more than one-half inch of the mouthpiece into your mouth. Touch the mouthpiece only with your lips, and be sure not to bite the mouthpiece with your teeth. When blowing into the instrument, it is important not to blow too hard. At first, play softly, because this will help you develop control. To begin a note, lightly tap your tongue against the roof of your mouth as if you were saying "tu."

Getting Acquainted with Music

Notes

Notes are used to indicate musical sounds. Some notes are long and others are short.

whole note	𝅝	gets 4 beats
half note	𝅗𝅥	gets 2 beats
quarter note	♩	gets 1 beat

Rests

Rests are used to indicate musical silence.

whole rest	▬	gets 4 beats
half rest	▬	gets 2 beats
quarter rest	𝄽	gets 1 beat

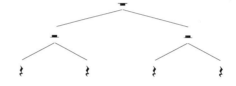

Staff

Music is written on a staff made up of five lines. Between each line there is a space.

line 5 ⟶ _____ ⟵ space 4
line 4 ⟶ _____ ⟵ space 3
line 3 ⟶ _____ ⟵ space 2
line 2 ⟶ _____ ⟵ space 1
line 1 ⟶ _____

Treble Clef

A clef is at the beginning of each line of music. The treble clef, also called the G clef, shows that the second line is the note G.

Notes on the Staff

E F G A B C D E F

Notes are named using the first seven letters of the alphabet (A B C D E F G).

The notes on the lines are:

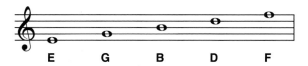

E G B D F

An easy way to remember this is the phrase "**E**very **G**ood **B**oy **D**oes **F**ine."

The notes in the spaces are:

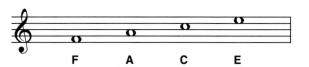

F A C E

The way to remember this is the word **FACE**.

Accidentals

An accidental raises or lowers the sound of a note. A sharp (♯) raises a note one half step. A flat (♭) lowers a note one half step. A natural (♮) cancels a sharp or flat. An accidental affects that note for the rest of that measure.

Measure
Music is divided into equal parts called measures.

Bar Lines
A bar line indicates where one measure ends and another begins.

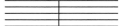

Double Bar
A double bar line, made of one thin line and one thick line, shows the end of a piece of music.

Time Signature

$\frac{4}{4}$ = 4 beats to a measure
$\frac{4}{4}$ = quarter note ♩ gets 1 beat

1 2 3 4   1 2 3 4   1 2 3 4

Ode To Joy (Easier Version)

This is an easy version of one of Ludwig van Beethoven's best-loved melodies.
Beethoven, who was born in Germany, is considered one of the most important composers in history.
For more information on this piece, see page 16. Keep the quarter notes even.

These are the notes you will need for this piece.

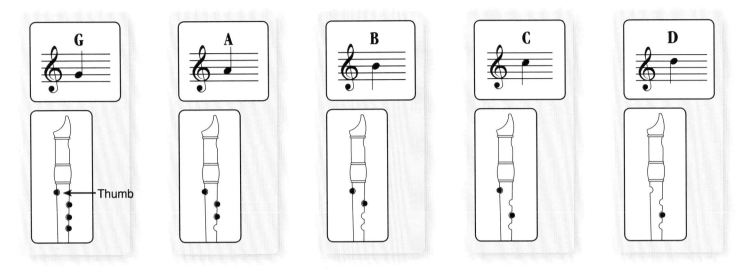

Ludwig van Beethoven

Count: 1   2   3   4   1   2   3   4   1   2   3   4   1   2   3   (4)

1   2   3   4   etc.

Theme from the "New World" Symphony

Antonin Dvořák was from Bohemia. He visited the United States in 1892 to teach music—this was just six years after the Statue of Liberty was assembled in New York. He was so inspired by American music that he wrote his "From the New World" symphony, and this melody is from the second movement.

New Note

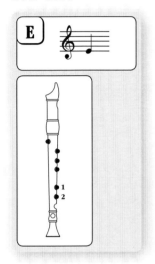

Antonin Dvořák

Barcarolle

A *barcarolle* is music in the style of songs sung by gondoliers (people who drive small boats called *gondolas*) in Venice, Italy. This barcarolle was written by German composer Jacques Offenbach for his opera *The Tales of Hoffman*.

New Time Signature

3 = 3 beats to a measure
4 = quarter note ♩ gets 1 beat

Dotted Half Note

When a dot follows a note, the length of the note is longer by one half of the note's original length.

A dotted half note gets three beats: 𝅗𝅥 . = 𝅗𝅥 + ♩

Jaques Offenbach

Finlandia

This is music from the national anthem of Finland.
It was written by Jean Sibelius, who is considered
one of the greatest Finnish composers.

New Note

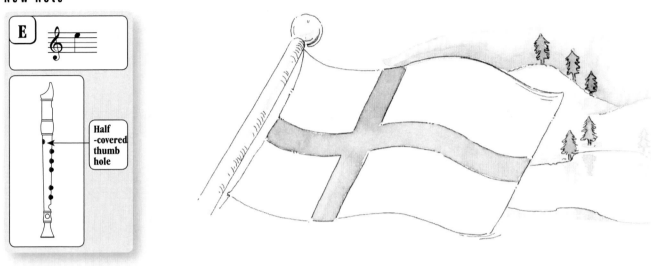

Quarter Rest

The quarter rest ⌡ gets one beat of silence.

Jean Sibelius

Theme from "Swan Lake"

The Russian composer Peter Ilyich Tchaikovsky composed two of the world's most popular ballets: *The Nutcracker* and *Swan Lake*. *Swan Lake* tells the story of a princess who is changed into a swan by an evil sorcerer.

New Note

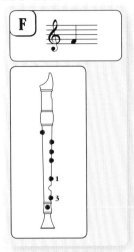

Ties

A tie ⌣ is a curved line that joins two or more notes of the same

pitch that last for the length of the combined note values ♩‿♩ .

Half Rest

A half rest ▬ gets two beats of silence.

Piotr Illych Tchaikovsky

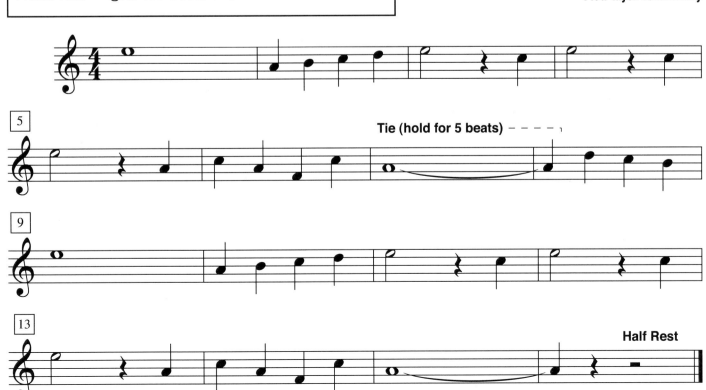

Can-Can

A *can-can* is a French dance that was popular in the nineteenth century. The German composer Jacques Offenbach included this can-can in his operetta *Orpheus in the Underworld*.

New Notes

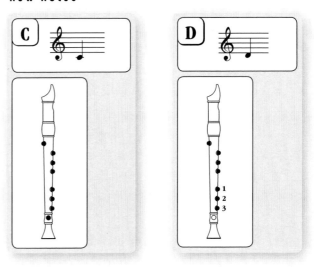

Tempo Marking

A tempo marking tells you how fast to play a piece. Tempo markings are placed above the first measure and are usually in Italian. *Allegro* indicates to play the piece fast.

Jaques Offenbach

Aria from "Don Giovanni" (Duet)

This is one of the most beautiful melodies by
Austrian composer Wolfgang Amadeus Mozart.
It is from his opera about the scheming knight,
Don Juan.

New Note

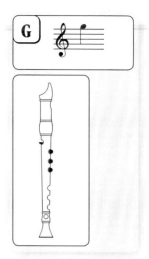

New Tempo Marking

Moderato means to play the
piece at a moderate speed.

Wolfgang Amadeus Mozart

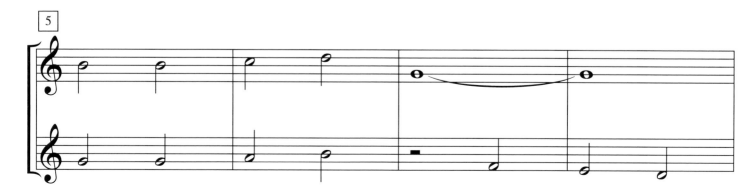

Theme from "William Tell"

This melody is from the overture to the opera *William Tell*
by the great Italian opera composer Gioachino Rossini.
The tune represents the calm following a fierce storm.

New Note

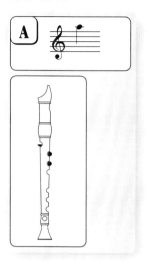

New Tempo Marking
Andante means to
play the piece slowly.

Gioachino Rossini

Musette (Duet)

A *musette* is a dance that imitates the sound of a bagpipe. The famous German composer Johann Sebastian Bach wrote this musette for a keyboard instrument.

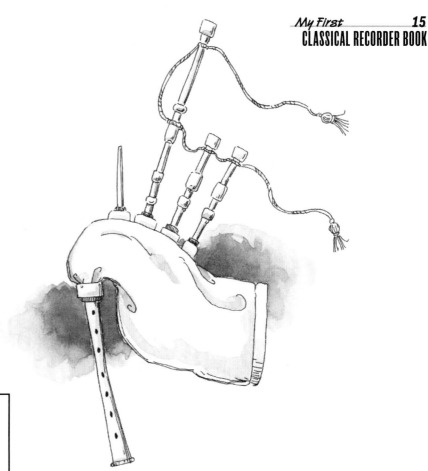

Repeat Sign
A repeat sign :|| means to go back to the beginning and play the music again.

Eighth Notes
There are two eighth notes played in the time of a quarter note.

Eighth notes look like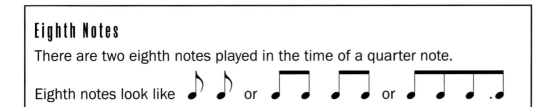

Johann Sebastian Bach

Repeat

Ode To Joy (Full Version)

This may be the most popular piece of classical music ever written. Beethoven composed this melody for his ninth symphony, which was the first symphony ever to include a large choir as part of the orchestra.

Common Time

$\frac{4}{4}$ time is often written as **C**, which stands for "common time."

Dotted Quarter Note

A dotted quarter note gets one and one-half beats.

It is the same length as a quarter note tied to an eighth note  .

Ludwig van Beethoven

Sonata Theme

In addition to being a wonderful composer, Wolfgang Amadeus Mozart was a fine pianist. This melody is from one of the many pieces he wrote for piano.

Wolfgang Amadeus Mozart

Merry Widow Waltz

A *waltz* is a dance with three beats to each measure. This waltz is from the opera *The Merry Widow*, by Hungarian composer Franz Lehar.

New Note

Franz Lehar

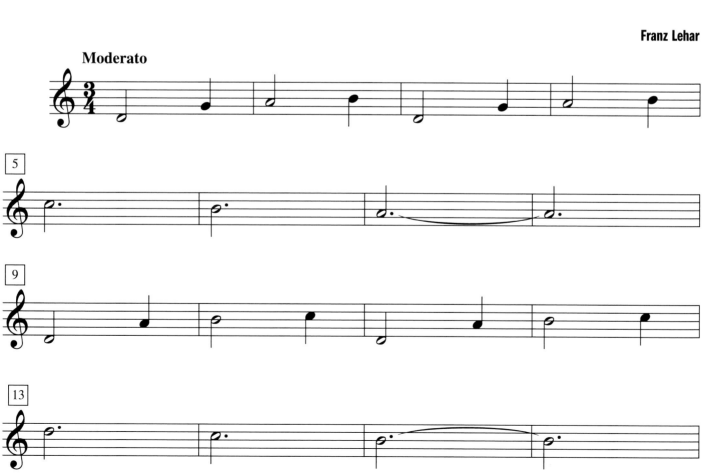

Eine Kleine Nachtmusik

This melody is from the first movement of a piece
Mozart wrote for string orchestra. The title literally
means "a little night music."

Wolfgang Amadeus Mozart

1812 Overture

This music is from Peter Ilyich Tchaikovsky's overture that musically describes the Russian defeat of Napoleon in 1812. At the end of the piece, the composer has actual cannons firing in time with the music!

Cut Time

This symbol $\mathory{C}$ indicates a time signature called Cut Time, which is the same as $\frac{2}{2}$.

2 = 2 beats to a measure
2 = half note gets one beat

The music looks the same as $\frac{4}{4}$, but it is played with a feel of two beats to the measure.

Piotr Illych Tchaikovsky

Theme from "Carmen"

French composer Georges Bizet wrote the opera *Carmen*,
which is set in Seville, Spain. Two of the main characters are
Carmen the Gypsy and a bullfighter named Escamillo.

New Note

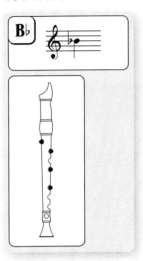

Georges Bizet

Theme from "Hansel and Gretel"

German composer Engelbert Humperdinck brings the fairy tale of Hansel and Gretel to life in this popular opera. The story follows the adventures of two children captured by a witch who lives in a gingerbread house in the forest.

Pickup Notes

When a piece of music doesn't begin on the first beat, it begins with an incomplete measure called a pickup. If the pickup is one beat long, the last measure will have only three beats in $\frac{4}{4}$, or two beats in $\frac{3}{4}$.

Engelbert Humperdinck

Lullaby

A *lullaby* is a song that is meant to be sung
to a baby in a cradle. The German composer
Johannes Brahms originally wrote this
melody for singer with piano.

Johannes Brahms

Theme from Beethoven's Fifth Symphony

Beethoven is probably best known for his fifth and ninth symphonies. This theme is from the opening of his fifth symphony. It is amazing how Beethoven created an entire movement of a symphony out of the first four notes.

Fermata

The fermata ⌢ tells you to hold the note longer than its normal length.

f is the symbol for *forte* which is Italian for loud.

p is the symbol for *piano* which is Italian for soft.

Ludwig van Beethoven

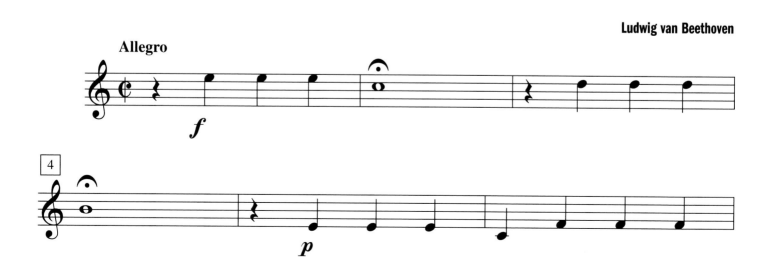

7

10
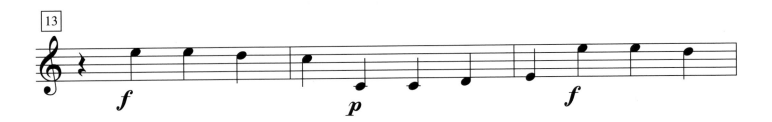

13

16

19

Dance of the Hours

The Italian composer Amilcare Ponchielli wrote many operas during his lifetime. His best-known composition is "Dance of the Hours" from the opera *La Gioconda*, which is about a traveling street singer from Venice.

Amilcare Ponchielli

Canon (Quartet)

Johann Pachelbel was a German composer who wrote music during the late seventeenth and early eighteenth centuries. A *canon* is a piece of music that is also called a *round*: One player (or *part*) begins to play the melody, and after a few measures, another part begins to play the same melody, note for note. This canon is a quartet, which means it is written for four parts.

Canon

A canon is a piece of music where there is more than one performer playing the same music, but they start at different times. For this piece, one person starts and continues playing. Each time you see the ❀ marking, another player starts at the beginning. Once everyone has had a chance to play through the entire piece, play the chord in the last measure with each player choosing one note.

Johann Pachelbel

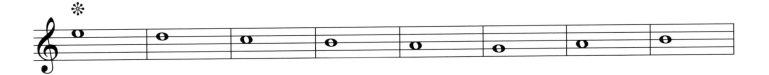

On the Beautiful Blue Danube

This is the melody from the popular waltz by Austrian composer Johann Strauss, Jr. The Danube is a great river that runs through Germany and France.

Johann Strauss Jr.

Complete Fingering Chart

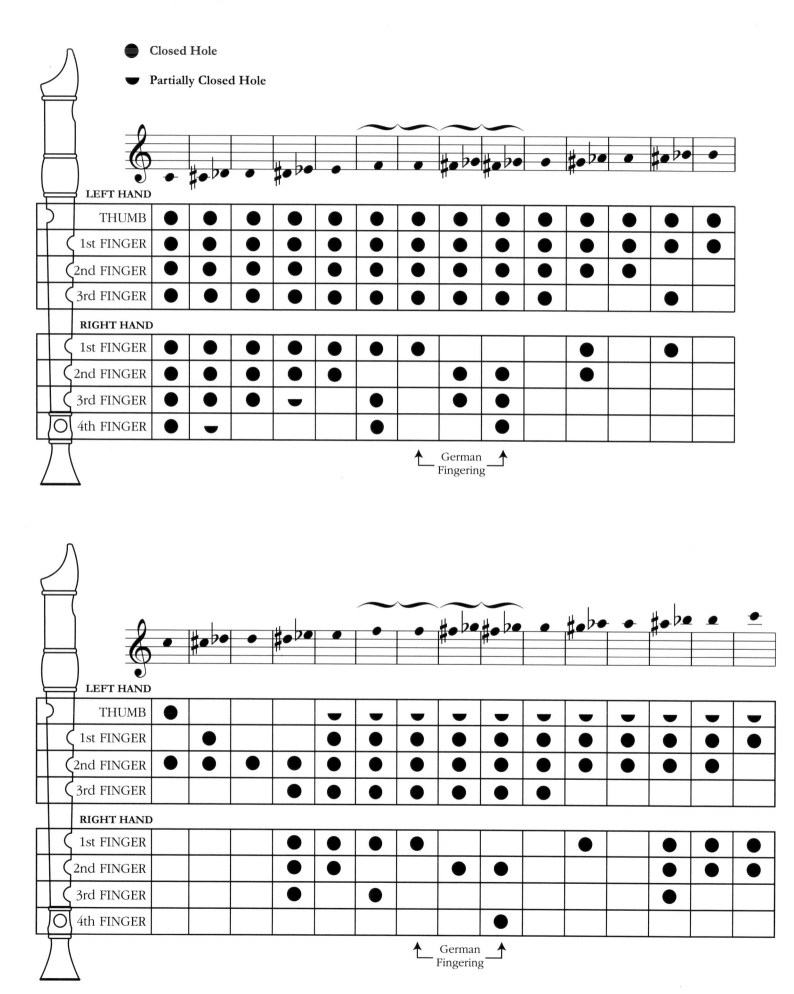

● Closed Hole

◗ Partially Closed Hole